THE GREEN BETWEEN THE EARS

SCRIPTOR HOUSE
The Epitome of Greatness

By Grizzly, Fred

A USA Golfer

Scriptor House LLC

2810 N Church St Wilmington, Delaware, 19802

www.scriptorhouse.com

Phone: +1302-205-2043

Published by Scriptor House LLC

Paperback ISBN: 979-8-88692-214-1

eBook ISBN: 979-8-88692-215-8

You will not be handed your golf ball on a silver spoon.
You must work hard to accomplish your goals.

Contents

PREFACE

The holes described in this writing may not be the same number on your particular round on a chosen course. The ideas will occur when you least expect them on any course. As you play through the great courses available, you will experience many types of obstacles. Your travels through each course on this road will become an exhilarating finish. You will bask in the sun and enjoy the gentle breezes of the day.

Remain energetic and you will overcome any obstacle thrown at you. This book will assist in the transition, enlighten your day and will give you many wonders to enhance this game of golf. Your goals are obtainable.

Do not fret, all movements have a way to show you the stronger points in your game. You are never too old to learn or refine the game to your liking. All of the technical studies will assist in guiding a game. Yet, the most knowledge gained is from you and your desire to remain with this game.

Practice, practice, and practice! If you are going to invest the time to get to the next level of expertise you must do these activities to better your shortcomings. The more you practice the more you achieve. If a golf trainer is involved, do not become intimidated, he or she might want you to keep your head down so you cannot see him or her laughing. Looking over a practice bucket of balls can cause anxiety. The real challenge comes when you actually reach the course. You will give each hit a steady aim to find that desired target.

This is your golfing book. It is your guide for successfully preserving the art of chasing a round object necessary for a delightful and vigorous life. Tomorrow's golf will create its own challenge. Do today what is necessary to gain respect as you go through a round of play.

Weathering the fairway storm:

1. Practice, Practice, Practice

2. Not a Numbers Game

3. Line Up Your Shots

4. Stay in the Zone

5. Calling the Shot

These tips shed light on how to stay calm in the storm and shoot straight down a fairway. These items will be expressed as you read the pages. It will fulfill your dream of following the round object around a field of beautifully manicured grass with many scattered obstacles along the side.

It's time to drive your way.

ACKNOWLEDGEMENT

For all golfers who have played the game with me. They have pointed out many issues of the game. These points became helpful in this writing. A golfer is never alone.

To the reviewers of the Free Lance Writers. Especially Gloria, Jean, Jon, and Jean. You all have been inspiring with your thoughts and encouragement.

APPROACH:

~

The winter weather has given way to lush green grass. It's golf time. You are about to participate in a sport that is enjoyed by thousands of people. This sport will challenge your every movement. Where you play is your choice. Can you handle the changes each stroke

v

provides you as you continue through the course? You will go into each game with your greatest expectations and find ways to place the little round object into its resting place.

You want to succeed each time you swing a golf club. How you succeed is determined by your approach and the desire to enjoy a game that is a challenge for most. What do you feel good about as you move around the course? If you cannot enjoy some happiness with the many strokes taken, then why do it? Some swings will be amazing, and you will want to continue experiencing this flow of enjoyment. It is really about the challenge of succeeding. Only you will know the answer. Disregard other players' thoughts about your game. Tune them out unless you are asking for guidance. You are the one who will be pleased with the outcome. Tomorrow will present more twists to the game and new challenges even if you are playing the same course. Your attitude will govern the outcome of each play.

Learn the many facts affecting the use of a club and your potential movements. You can practice and practice but without actual experience on the course practice does little. The level of play you want to reach determines your practice routine. You can avoid surprises by setting the tone each time you approach the green. Misconceptions can continue if you do not think about what you should do. You may hear inaccurate comments from other players or you might misjudge your actual hitting abilities to remain in the fairway.

We all have patterns of behavior that will continue on the course. This activity will be fine as long as you understand what you want to accomplish. Preparing your game plan becomes beneficial to your future enjoyment of the game. You make the choice but remember your desire to enjoy this exciting game. Become aware of your surroundings and change your actions. Your positive movements will afford you the happiness necessary to survive each future beautiful day in the outdoors on the golf course. Reevaluate your personal self. Then you can become that satisfied person you wish to see in the mirror.

Budgeting is used on each roll of life. This process examines the many facets of how we approach life's issues outside of the golf plays and how we strive to accomplish a satis-factory end to those events. Thus, in the wealth of golfing ideas to be learned becomes a life structure that can build your character in another viewpoint. Don't stress out on a misguided shot. You will make an adjustment after each stroke, just as in life you make the adjustments to handle your events. Life will provide many benefits gained by the changes you need to make. Budgeting gives each a time to examine details of the game and life game. This budgeting process will help identify how each club in your bag should work through your play on the course. We approach a tee box with the idea of gaining a respect of where the round object will come to rest. Another budgeting process is your dedication with continued success and a watchful eye of all swings you take that will move you forward to the desired result. As you continue to study this game you will find more processes that guide any changes you wish to make.

Game play issues will be presented as the game goes forward through the round of golf. Each stroke with your tools will make this a very enjoyable day. It is time to begin the round as you have practiced doing those things that make you feel ready.

** Make the game fun and examine your self being.
Get ready for that call to the "first tee." **

HOLE # 1

~

You start this position by placing a tee into the ground (at your height level) and set a ball on top of this stick. You gaze into the future as each shot will do its own wild process with your help. You look over the fairway from side to side and do realize the potential of the round object to move straight forward.

Some fairways have on the right or left side a long row of trees. You ask yourself what happens if the ball sails to the right after the hit? Where will you go either in search of the missing white object or just re-hit and hope your concentration effort survives the next test. Some long hitters want to sail the ball over those trees as the landing green is slightly to the right after the trees. They are modest and say to themselves nothing will go wrong with the hit and you will survive the passage to the open area.

Therefore, no matter your expertise as a golfer you can find yourself either in the muck or safely on the fairway for the next hit. Some golfers - beginners or average players - will want to travel into the trees and find that lost object. Surprise once you get in the middle of the trees and look around for your golf ball you are amazed at the quantity of white, yellow, and other colors lay undisturbed on the ground. You start it just takes a few minutes to pick up the objects and find your pockets bulging with golf balls to be played again. Most average golfers can reuse these recycled objects in the future of their game.

A golf club is taken out of the bag. This tool is chosen to be the correct item to use for this distance to strike the round object. The tee is approached with the end of the stick and a vision is provided. The tool is swung back to the summit then brought forward to release the ball from its perch. The swing swayed from straight and the ball went far right and landed in the tall rough and the trees. Just as a technique routine goes astray you land in the muck. You now go hunting for the great white.

A review of the landing area causes a strong examination of the process that caused this action. What now do you do to make a corrective measure for the future? Your concen-tration effort must be sincere to make the next movement to succeed and keep the ball on course. These future swings of a club with a metal end must move in the direction to cause less pain on the desired result. It becomes time to approach the next shot. The process of examining the round object begins with regards to the whereabouts of the landing area to the green. How can you move this object to the desired result of placing the object into the cup to finish the hole?

** Push forward and review each approach to reach
your goals you have set for success. **

HOLE # 2

~

You have successfully completed your first attempt to reach the goal of going "plunk into the hole." Let's begin the next approach with the same enthusiasm as you used to move through the fairway to the green.

This time you begin the review as you look forward over the fairway. On the left side of the fairway there are several sand traps, on the right side is a large tree standing in the way of a beautiful shot. You must guide your hit object through the narrow passage to reach the green. This hole is nearly two hundred and fifty yards longer. You will have more opportunities to strike the little round object to reach its goal. There is a curve in the fairway.

The challenge begins as you set the small pedestal in the ground that will hold the round object. You pull from your pocket one of the previously lost objects to set upon the wood stick. Oh, how nice it feels not to strike a ball from your own supply. This ball looks so shiny, as though it has never been hit before. Probably was stricken only once, lost and not gathered by a previous golfer.

You pull a long stick from your bag with a large head on the end. This device gives you the sense that based on the size you will be able to hit the round object much further. Only to your surprise it fails to go that extra distance. The big story pops right at you "Oh my, I am in the sand." Again, you think about what caused you to end at the current landing point. This story explains the many facets of how a stick with an iron head will be moving the white object from the sand to a landing closer to the green surface. Fortunately, the ball did not go deep into the sand making it a more difficult shot to go forward.

You will choose a club that will glide over the sand when striking the round object and making it an easier placement to the next landing. That will work only if you have accomplished this type of shot many times in the past. Usually with the early years and possibly later years of golfing experience, this movement of the round object just barely goes over the top of the sand trap. If hit strongly it may roll a much shorter distance away from this hazard than expected. Sometimes the next movement amazes you as the ball sails in a straight line towards its goal. You landed just short of the green. The next hit is then known as a "chip shot", usually less than forty yards from the final resting place for this hole.

A key factor in this golf technique is developing the confidence that your hits will move positively forward.

HOLE # 3

~

You move away from the past green and look at the tee box for the upcoming hole. If you are walking, it will be a short climb up a small hill. Otherwise, the cart riders will zip around to the starting point. This all depends on the expertise level of the golfer. You can use either the blue, white, gold, or red tee boxes to hit your golf ball. Each box behind the red box adds more yardage to the drive. Some golfers may prefer the blue tee box for more excitement and extra yards to hit the ball. Especially if you are having difficulties hitting the preferred distance.

A different approach to regain the confidence in hitting the round object with greater ease. You will become surprised as you approach the upcoming hole when using this strategy. Other golfers in your group may wonder what you are doing. You and only you need this option to make your game a huge benefit. They will be shaken when you swing and amaze them with this approach. Now the time has come to set up the stick in the ground and place your round object on top. You take out the appropriate club to be swung in the direction of the desired result.

After the hit, you are in the middle of the fairway. The analysis begins in sizing up the approach to the magnificent "green." As so many times in the past, your drives lead you to a point of comfort. You always examine each future hit with strong confidence and thought as if you own the next motion. Your decision will allow the golfer in you to do it. Once the approach has been examined and owned the review process is completed. The short iron will be used to hit the white object to seek its direction to the destination chosen. It sails ever softly and easily to land within inches of the designated hole. The steps taken will enhance the growth you experience in taking these "baby golf steps" to give credit its true respect.

You as a golfer will improve your efforts with each drive and approach encountered.

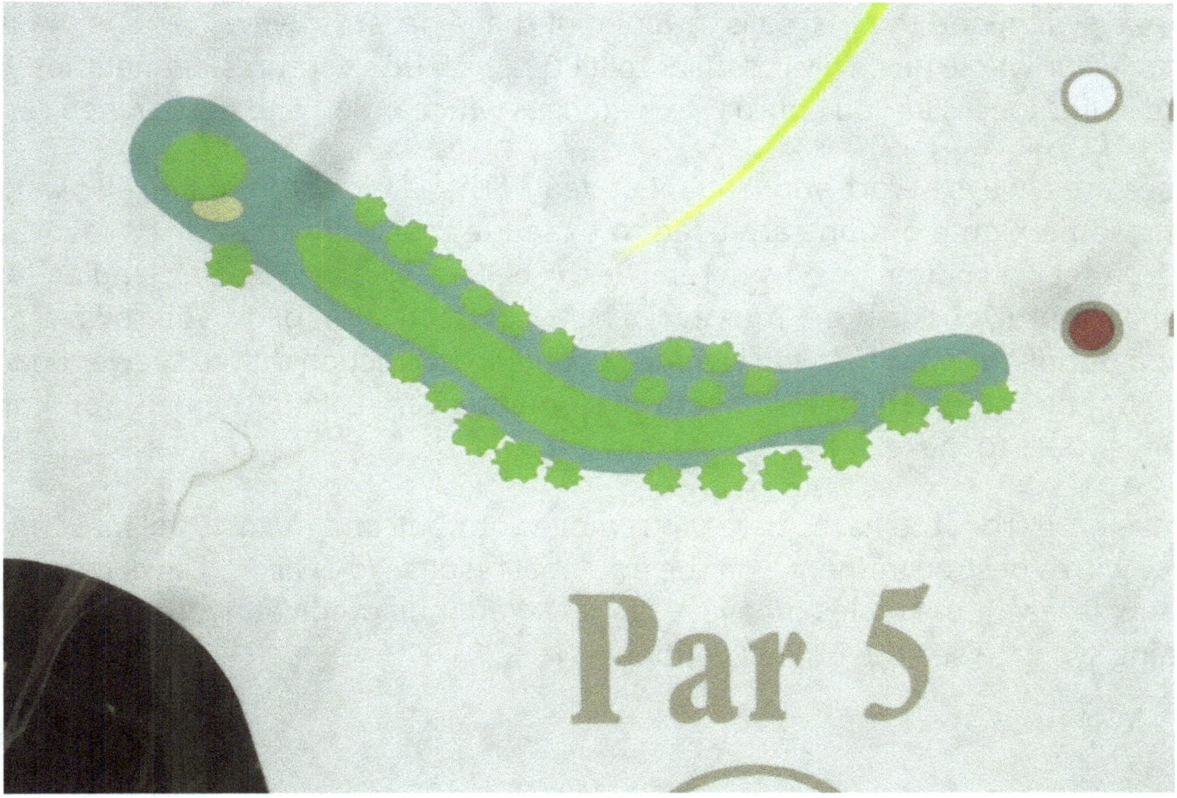

HOLE # 4

You can examine the golf score card for the layout of this hole. Your findings show this hole is a good dogleg to the right, a fairly large bend in the fairway to the green. You look forward and see water on the left and various sand landings on the right plus trees and taller grass on the left. You must select numerous options to overcome these obstacles. You always examine each experience.

You take a swing, and the ball sails into one of these hazards. Never let one messed up shot spoil your whole day. This is similar to all types of life's ventures. Sometimes you will succeed in life's turns as you approach challenges with caution and determined resolve.

Surprises are always before you. You must deal with many hurtles in life, also in the golf field the same. Some options are used to examine the landings of one's favorite little critter. You seek an option on how to remove the ball from its aggravating landing site. This decision is left to your desires. You revoke a strict directive to follow your own reachable path. You decide the view that you want to succeed in a direction that has fewer headaches and will be the preferred image of your placement after striking the ball. You know the decision is yours to make.

You strike hard from the hazard area to remove your ball and make it sail into the future pathway with a desired influence on the potential results. You will find a way to overcome the many different obstacles on every fairway. You must dedicate your movement to a refreshing swing to see the brighter outlook.

Seeking an approach is like heading into the rough and finding many surprises under the ground cover.

That is where the little creature has crawled

HOLE # 5

~

You arrive at the next "Tee Box" to plan your next event. There is a finish to this forward motion. As you address the round object and look down the fairway, you will visualize the flight - - the carefree flight of your round object. This flight will take off as you make a large backward swing to propel the club forward. This advance the little round object toward its future destination. The way it will travel depends on your concentration efforts. Hope and a prayer will propel the white object to the desired landing area. Remembering as you watch you have a feeling of controlling the chosen landing because you chose the path.

You will proceed with your plans to succeed as you move forward the required motion for play. You strike the object with new adventures. You observe all plant growth surrounding the fairway as you look forward and side to side to visualize the path. You disrupt your comfort zone by swaying right or left from the appointed destination. Then, you must address the hard decisions as your special round object lays waiting for some movement. Go seek your path.

Make it a triumphant victory. Leave the worry within your inner heart.

You must strike with a smooth motion.

HOLE # 6

~

The events that send each golfer in a direction to gain perspective of the game's activities are considered humongous. Following a round object from the starting area with a small stick stuck into the ground starts these activities. From this tee you will swing forward with the greatest of ease and see how far you travel without major stress. The greatest distance traveled is straight down the fairway. Once hit, the round object is sent on a path that overlooks the ground below as it travels the distance.

The ground cover below the ball path can be green grass, and other obstacles such as a track, water, rocks, sand, trees, and tall grasses. All of these items can be in the flight path on the actual fairway or over the shortest distance to the goal. Sailing through the air allows you the time to feel a course changing behavior. Do we excel in our activities of play?

Which direction have you sent the message? Are you building lifelong habits by setting things on a course that allows forgiveness? Your round objects will land and roll to the destination you strive to achieve. Your relationships are being built from your observation of the surroundings.

Your current landing area keeps you returning for another round as you stay focused on the short-term goals. Stay the course! You maintain a written document of your actions known as a scorecard. This card is accurate because anything less will create a misrepresentation of your play. You, and only you will know how the next practices or play will identify your shortcomings. This document is for your use and future examination.

You have learned what it takes to guide your round object to its destination. The ground is green and lush from all the care it received. This allows each person to proceed without interruptions. The lowered stress will give you an evening of delight as you reflect on the day's activity.

Go forward by striking evenly through the swing.

Be not afraid from all the knowledge received to find that path of pursuit to clearly move to higher rewards of this game.

HOLE # 7

This hole is considered short in yardage. Therefore, a smaller-angled club face size will be the desired striking tool. Some golfers may use a wedge or a nine iron to approach the end result. Others will use a five or six iron. The type of striking tool will depend on your experience level for this yardage.

No pedestal (tee or mud) is required for this movement. Your desired round object is placed on the ground. The fun and excitement of this adventure and your training will enable you to really hit the round object "in or near the cup." A real challenge for this approach is the confidence you must retain to hit the round object.

There is a great tendency to leave the ball short of the green because you know it is a short distance and you do not use the normal force to sail your ball to its preferred landing zone. The short-distance golf holes always leave you questioning why you use half speed to arrive at the desired place. Rely on your training when you approach this type of hole. Using a different utensil from your bag results in a greater misstep with your approach.

All golf tools have a purpose for distance and exact use. Remembering what each tool is designed to accomplish will create a better result. The swing remains normal as you go backward and upward with the tool and bring it forward to strike your small round object the same way each time. These swings will build the complete golfer in each situation.

Always go the distance.

HOLE # 8

~

You arrive on this hill to observe the next fairway and what it has to offer as a desired approach. You have completed many adventures during the previous golfing holes. Your experiences have gained a knowledge base that will grow with each new stroke of the club. Your refreshed desire will entertain you throughout the upcoming play.

This hole differs from all others you have tried because it remains the longest fairway. You always need new challenges to develop your talents. Your approach remains intact from everything you have learned gained from the previous experiences of the day. Observation of this fairway gives a new insight to the word "cornfields." Yes, you have a long stretch of agricultural activity. Some courses are built near farming ventures. They add to the appeal.

It is true that, you can hear the corn growing and speaking to you. Just listen!! Then, when your ball is sent sailing into the field, be not afraid. Just observe the level of talk that is occurring. Someone is listening to your every movement down the fairway. If you desire, you may go into the field and determine where your ball has landed. This walk will be venturous as the unknown will become enlightening. You observe the ground level filled with numerous white and colored objects left behind by others who do not take an adventurous stroll. Where is the curiosity you have from all other walks of life you encounter? Later in the golfing and growing seasons you are being observed and watched by many **"corn stalks with two ears".** The stories these ears tell will be a wide awakening, as the other players that also landed and words these players used. These words will sharpen your talking skills after the round is over. Listen carefully!

Find those obstacles that will create adventure with each movement you encounter through life's activities.

Listen intensively.

HOLE # 9

~

Now is the time to review your confidence level and your desired results. The activity during the first half of play is an amazing feat. Relax and let your swing do the work. The key factor with any golfing technique is developing confidence as you move the golf ball. The round object will sail in the direction hit.

When you have played for hours and find the round object is "not obeying your desired movement," look at your approach style. Pull from your pocket another round ball that may obey you when struck. Move around on the "tee box" to find a location that better suits your hitting abilities. It will not take long to feel the control and the ball will not stray.

Spraying hits left or right will have a huge effect on your ability to remain in the middle of the fairway. This will have a negative impact on your potential to lead the ball toward the landing locations. A sailing ball feels drained after you have made an impact on it throughout the day.

It is important to remember that golf balls don't have a good survival rate. Many factors can change the shape and landing surfaces of your object. Your hitting abilities may place a cut or slice on the surface of the ball. Going out of bounds and landing in the rough may scratch or dent the surface. Landing in water may attract undesirable matter to this surface.

Go forward with your review of the approach for the desired result. You will hear the familiar **"clunk"** when the ball drops into the hole.

Let's take a short break and enjoy refreshments before beginning the second half of your round.

RESTING TIME: BETWEEN FIRST HALF AND SECOND HALF OF A ROUND

Take the extra steps to insure your satisfaction and success. Your personality and interpersonal communication skills are two of the biggest assets when trying to strike a round object. You are drawn to golfing because you do not give up at the first sign of a challenge. You know it's going to be a tough road.

Your attributes to perseverance in part to being a highly independent person who believes in practice, patience and persistence. You love to assist the round object and you are a problem solver to move this object to a desired resolution. You are passionate about learning and being successful to the game when you thought there could not be success and no chance to thrive.

As countless people have said, your personal experiences and changes make you laugh, cry, be amazed at where you are right now and go after every dream you want. Become energetic, resourceful, athletic, motivated, and motivational. You are a golfer who hates to fail, you embrace failure not as a loss, but as opportunity to educate and endure this game. Each golfer has heard stories about the power of friendship and the lengths each player will go to encourage others as they fight to reclaim the green as their own.

A disability does not display your personal health situation. You may have limited length of hand strength and movement. Pick golf as a sport and your belief will be that you can excel no matter what disability you are presented. Each type of disability will present the challenge to succeed in this sport.

You begin a regimen of training to develop the skills needed. During the play presentation, thus completed, you recall how some of the early training efforts lacked promise. You remember the time you duffed the ball at impact.

In the practice presentations, you provided a demonstration of the technique using a small target set at the rear of the platform, the "tee box", where you will deliver the ultimate swing. You will learn how to keep a low-key delivery adding inspirational stories which are interspersed with funny life experiences. This driver technique is called "remain focused on your target."

Taking a break after a brutal first half of play is most encouraging and inspires the golfer to be ready for the second half of activity. Remove any negative thoughts of the first half round. It will delay you in obtaining the attitude needed to play the second half of the round. If a golfer does more than is required then you are considered the best you can be at the time of play, if not you are just a player.

Let us now strike forward to enter the next stage of play, the second half of the round.

HOLE # 10

~

You move from the clubhouse to the awaiting tee box. You look around and see players moving their clubs around their bodies, exercising for the next approach. You are preparing a warm sendoff of the little round object to its next destination. This preparation has loosened those tired muscles created from the time at the refreshment stand.

You assess the next fairway design and future execution of your play. This will give you less chance to dwell on the emotional flow of your past swings. You examine the post with the layout of this airway. It shows a dogleg left halfway down the plush green grass. This will be a more delicate shot. You have sliced your swings in the past and now on this fairway you must take the same approach with a small slice to be recognized as part of the actual swing.

You set the ball upon its pedestal and step back a few feet to observe the future forward motion. You are ready to take a stance next to the little round object. Set the club face just behind this pedestal and look down the fairway one last time. This look gives you the enjoyment of your future drive and what it will accomplish.

The club begins to retreat backwards and upwards to its height and you push forward with a direct downward motion to strike the intended object. Wow!!!! That little round object travel is unlike any you have moved in the past. You observe its path as it flows gently to the landing area.

You stand tall on the tee box, proud of your accomplishment with this swing. You jump with joy that you really can complete an activity. Your practices have paid off. What an upbeat moment!

Perfection was pursued and you see that attaining it was possible.

HOLE # 11

This hole is long. You must determine which club from your large bag should be used first, second and third. The fairway is straight forward with no curves to cause any obstacles to pop-up when hit straight away. The power of concentration is used with each swing. If not used, the rough areas will jump into your path. You must seize the opportunity.

Examination of the tee box has provided the emphasis of how well you can achieve your goal. Going to the "gold tee box" and hitting the object like there is no tomorrow and hope the little round object gets past the red tee box is exhilarating.

Based on the previous hole results you can swing effortlessly to another wonderful ending. These thoughts begin to rumble through your golfing vocabulary. The golfer in you wants to reach an excellent outcome just to feel great again.

Your decision is using the "blue tee box." This is the most reasonable approach as your experience does fluctuate emphatically. You reach into the pocket full of round objects and choose one that will be sent on its merry way. You turn forward to the thoughts of the future flight of this object. You understand the need to stay positive and let go of bad shots.

Just as in life learning means letting go of any mistakes.
The light switch has been flipped. Letting go is a wonderful thing.

HOLE # 12

~

You have arrived at the outer edge of the green. You look at the lay of the green. There are many slight slopes, and you must read them to determine the future roll of your small object. You see several bumps rising over the area. You must get the ball to the next level without letting it roll backwards.

The next motion gets frustrating if your stroke is slow in developing. A firm hit can be accomplished. Your little object will roll smoothly to the final destination, especially if you think positively and block out any disturbance in your mind.

The goal is being set for what must be done to move forward. You line up the putter behind your little ball. This next roll will find all the curves in the lay of the land. With a keen eye, you set in motion your stroke. The ball moves forward turning left and right toward the goal.

Surprise! You have overlooked one slope, and the ball continues to roll away from its final destination. Now, you must reanalyze your preparation. Difficulties always drop in front of you when you least expect them.

A movement of distress will occur at a moment's notice. Be strong and do not despair. You can overcome. You set in motion the necessary action to move your round object through the next step.

You need to think about the follow through of your stroke. Making the difference is the movement of your club without any hesitation in the delivery. These movements on this green are deceptively simple and endlessly complicated. You take hold of this idea and move into the recovery stage.

The end is near as you begin the test of moving your round object to its resting place. The distance to cover is fourteen feet. You drop to your hands and knees to observe this area of land. You focus on the round hole as you look over this smooth green area.

There appears to be no barriers of curves or inclines in this portion of the green. So, a smooth run to the end is set in motion. You arise from the surface and place the putter in hand and set it behind your object and see the path to reach your goal. The movement of the putter is slightly backwards and move forward as a firm contact is made and the ball moves effortless to the sound of "plunk" into the hole. You survived this episode of a challenging game.

Fun in this game is the determination to win at the end of a hole
and the patience to entertain all positive movement
that await your future play.

HOLE # 13

~

You arrive at the tee box with great enthusiasm. This event will be another challenge as you observe a vast area of obstacles - thick grasses, tall grasses, and water. The distance is nearly three-quarters of the path to the next green. The area below the flight path is covered with many lost round objects. You worry about losing your favorite round object.

The club chosen helps move your round object to the landing area. A smooth swing will accomplish the expected goal for this hole. Your ball must rise quickly in order to sail over the grasses without connecting to the ground cover.

The ball is placed on the ground or a pedestal that will assist in moving to the destination. You begin your normal preparations of setting in motion the movement of the club to strike your little round object. The ball is just below and forward of your feet.

Upon completion of the review, you make the ball move forward with a swift and strong swing. After the hit, you walk into the rough area and locate many fallen round objects. These new-found balls will replenish your lost supply.

There are no golfers close behind you so you continue hunting as you begin the walk toward the green. As an amateur in this game you begin to fill your pockets. It is amazing how many of the lost items have been hit only once.

Many golfers do not take the time to observe the land that their balls have dropped in for a visit. Just like walking in the woods you see things that are not seen because people normally try to walk around any obstacles.

Life is full of obstacles you would rather side step than go directly up to the subject matter and discuss or observe the particular event. In many cases, a person creates the difficulty by not confronting the issue.

This will make unhappy days ahead. Get through the event and search for solutions that create a less stressful future. Memory of a tragic placement of a golf shot is almost impossible to recreate without understanding its original movements.

Turn a disaster into a positive activity.
Greater enjoyment will surpass any long-term negative effects.

Pathway is the Zone

HOLE # 14

This is the time to stay in the zone, which is straight forward. Everyone has a zone that extends from the tee box at roughly a 90-degree angle. The golfer instruction is simple. Do not strike anything that will go outside the zone.

This helps minimizing the many hits on the ball. A shot may go straight up and land behind you or near you. This identifies the placement of your round object excessively too high on the pedestal. Search out the target and see where it is sitting and this will make the hitting effort less painful.

Always focus your eyes on the sitting position of your round object. This helps your future movement to remain on target. The size of the area from left to right will vary depending on your approach stage. This stage overlooks a large oval or tear-drop pattern. No wayward movement is best for a most direct approach to your goal.

Once the ball is stricken, its movement forward will continue to close the gap from start to finish. A thumb rule of golf is shared by many golfers to estimate whatever length you think your distance will be. Then you must double the power of the hit to arrive at the distance originally projected. As you continue learning the game, this power factor is less of an issue. The smooth swing backward and forward to the object will result in greater distance obtained.

You are the farmer of your ball creating the light-bulb effect of a future path.

HOLE # 15

A look at the standing plaque displaying the hole directions and obstacles on the fairway will give you a greater feeling for a renewed experience. You begin your approach to the tee box and placement of the little round object. A strong look down the fairway identifies any obstacles to be experienced.

You begin the swing and hit the ball with the force needed to send the little round object on its way over the lush, trimmed green grass on the fairway. The golf ball landing is always a mystery. Observation of this path shows the ball hitting a large tree. After its hit the ball lands safely on the fairway. Amazing!

This tree was a saving value for the roll of the object. The ball was originally heading for a hazard near the outside area of the fairway. You will seek comfort in the best landing possible. You must be living right at this time. Many obstacles are presented to a person daily and how you survive each is and will remain a mystery.

Practice and work activity bring about positive results. You reflect on various concerns that may scare you and offer happiness at the same time. You are relieved with this experience and offer gratitude that continued movement and discipline helps each forward movement life presents.

Traveling thru the fairways of life's many courses gives great relief that

you can reach a defined goal of opportunities each round sets before you.

Seek the adventure and take the chances.

HOLE # 16

~

You have broken your concentration as you try to return to the surface. Many things have come before you and make it difficult to survive the present. How you approach this subject area with dignity will become your healthy way to remain on the fairway.

Striking forward, it will show your true spirit to begin anew. The rocket club, the one with the most speed and is less accurate, will usually spray the shots to the right or to the left and takes you off track of the main goal. You want the ball to go the distance and you lose the concentration effort. You must restart your golfing efforts. Through the days of your life you are permitted to throw away the obstacles that toss you into the rough. Do not be afraid. Seek the positive approach. You will be grateful for this action.

You are eliminating those tools in your bag, so a new life can begin. Become confident by using a new tool to strike the round object straight down the fairway. Dreaming is one of the first steps that allows you to set up the direction for your round object to travel. Remain positive with your approach that seeks a greater more graceful flight of your round object.

This flight of the ball will show, when using a camera, the sight below the path of the round object as it travels. The distance above the surface traveled does offer you the enthusiasm within your plans to proceed towards a brighter future. The greatest adventure is hitting the future target.

Set the determined path by giving the greatest benefit to accomplishing the strongest goal.

HOLE # 17

~

The ball landed on the upside of a hill on the fairway. Unable to see the next landing area, you must develop a plan for the future direction. Let's picture what is the pursuit. You knew from the beginning this fairway is long. Unexpected rolls of the ball will stop you short of fulfilling your first plan.

Walk to the crest of the hill and view the fairway and formulate a vision for the next flight. The idea you know is the visibility limits of the potential landing space. Do not let your emotions rule the next challenge no matter the situation.

You should be thankful for where you are and know where you should go with the next strike of the round object. Pure concentration is a must in this game. How you accomplish this process is determined by your actions. Happiness with your decision will provide a warm and encouraging end to this current challenge.

You have made the forward movement of the club and now start the walk to visualize where the landing space is located. You reached the top of the hill and are surprised how far your efforts resulted in an amazing hit. The dedication you provide gives proof of what an amazing golfer you have become. You are now reaching into your bag for greater satisfaction of this game.

The golfing routine always offers a challenge.
You must overcome.
Relief is around the corner.

HOLE # 18

Dreams for this Golfer

You have reached the final tee box of this journey. You have been successful following through the obstacles and remain on the green fairways. Your challenge is straight ahead as you set up the object to be stricken. You pull a handle from the bag. This tool has a device on the end to strike your little round object. You place the club behind the round object. You make a concentrated effort to line up the target stretching to the finish zone area. Then you bring your arms back with the club rising up above your head as you prepare to swing down at a fast pace. This will send the ball on a flight pattern toward the finish zone. It is a beautiful sight to see, as you watch the round object move forward without hesitation to its goal.

As all golfers will do, you reach into your bag and bring forth the imagination that guides all efforts. Stay the path and leave all obstacles behind as the ball will sail effortlessly to its destination.

The ground underneath your path seems to be covered with beauty and grace. The ball flies over the peaceful quietness of the path. The round object will land with grace and roll a great distance. This will set up the approach to the finish line. You have reached a goal that became your destiny and award.

Achieving your dreams is the key to a happy life. So, write down a dream and go for it. When you achieve it, **Celebrate!**

The wealth of your experience through this journey has been exhilarating.

All dreams can be accomplished when you concentrate

REFLECTIONS FROM THE CONCLUSION OF A ROUND OF GOLF

~

You began the tour around a large course. It started by placing, a beautiful little round object on top of a pedestal on a box of green grass. You created the excitement in this game by your play.

You draw from a bag a stick with a large device on its end. This device is lined up with the round object. You look forward and envision what will happen to the round object as it is hit and goes the distance straight away. Your mind is free of any obstacles. You have cleared the way for smooth sailing around the course.

You are pleased as all issues are pushed aside and you are free to see an outstanding landing plus a good roll. This event began your venture through the activities presented in your pursuit. You begin to process the beauty of each hit. You envision obstacles on your path. Throw away any negative thoughts and jump forward and above those creatures. They only want to affect your feelings.

Let's begin your own tour. Experience the activity of a golfer's life. Examine your beginning so you will gain relief within that tour. The journey never stops. Make time to aim higher and reach farther those goals that will help you finish the round.

Be realistic with your dreams and guiding them to your potential growth in the field. You are always learning. Broaden your horizons with each new drive forward. The gauges one uses to fulfill the success are determined by your ability to grow with each step.

Stay on top of your golf goals, and everything will work out. Your training is not bound by your physical limits. Your knowledge of the sport expands your abilities. Each goal can be a small existence at first as you get familiar with seeing the results. Once you achieve a goal strike out and become brave with new challenges.

There should never be random hits. You must always try to process these hits within your own ability. You dream of an important round. You, and no one else, can develop the mechanics. What it takes to move a white round object through all its travels. Reflect on the past trials and tribulations. Determine why the white round object did not travel as you predicted.

Many demands are placed on you, and each must be analyzed. You must be truthful to yourself during all of the shots. Maintain the fun. Plan these activities and do not overdo expectations. You have gained the secret during this process. Look at a rainy day as time for reflection.

Somewhere now, someone is standing at a window with coffee in hand, watching the sun climb over the horizon to awaken the sky. Someone else is enjoying a beautiful sunset. Each person has a challenge before him or her or has completed a challenge for the day. A person lives in the moment.

You enjoy the future and reflect on the past. Using your resources wisely has always been a challenge. You all want to provide for your current and future needs. Be wise in preparing for tomorrow's game. What you do with each event is a major task. You must view each day with gratitude and stay tuned to your adventures. You will strike forward in accomplishing your dreams and goals.

You are going to hit a positive note and raise your positive thinking to greater heights. Each golfer can make the future more powerful as you reflect upon the opportunities that surround your environment. Be rich in good works, ready to give, and willing to share and build a good foundation for the time to come.

You will be surprised as you analyze those individuals around you. Their growth in this sport will amaze you. It does not take a well-versed person to help others as they tackle this spectacular sport. There will be many occasions to assist other golfers to improve their abilities.

One of the missions of this book was to spread the belief that true beauty is defined by kindness, confidence and love. Never waver from your own mission, touching lives through meaningful stories. Voices from a warrior can teach life lessons in this great sport.

People in our nation are encouraged to "rock what you got." We are reminded to ignore the new wrinkles on ourselves, to love ourselves, and cherish our health no matter what age. You will shine with the beauty and love so brightly that you will never notice any non-conformities.

You refuse to wear a substitute player because each is beautiful without it. Through all this motivation you learn lessons about yourself, your craft, and your life. You make these efforts to give of yourself and to others as you gain a positive attitude.

If you do not go after what you want, you will never have it. If you do not ask, the answer will always be no. If you do not step forward, you will always be in the same place. These maxims apply to the greens and fairways, also. In the end, the golfer learns to make this game an exciting experience.

You associate with people who care about the game. As your relationships with other golfers grow, you discover that you share much in common. They give you the encouragement to follow through with each swing. One learns so much about the game through all the companionship you have with others. You must be trustworthy to be a worthy golfer friend.

Another key lesson is believing in yourself even when no one else does. You have never met a successful golfer who has not had to overcome either a little or a lot of adversity. So, who says that you cannot accomplish your golfing goals? Who says that you are not tougher, better, smarter, harder working and more able than your golfer friends?

It does not matter if people say you cannot do it. The only thing that matters is if you believe it. You have learned that you cannot go it alone. It is teamwork that helps this effort. It is a collection of people who respect each other and are committed to each other's success. The beautiful part of teamwork is that it offers you the opportunity to use your own special talents and abilities.

One last thing put some fun and creativity into golfing. You can take your golf relationships seriously but you should never take yourself too seriously. Supremely confident people worry little about being the coolest, smartest, most admired golfer in the room. They understand that putting others first will move them to the forefront.

They have learned some of golfer's most important lessons. There is a rainbow of hope after every storm. In the end you regret the chances you did not take, the relationships you were afraid to have and the decisions you waited too long to make. Learn from any mistakes. Be grateful for second chances and forgiving golfer friends. **Make your golfing life a best seller. Golfers are always working toward a more fulfilling life.**

You have to keep going, no matter what new challenges the day holds. When times are tough, in order to get through the day, you need to get through the next thing, whatever it is. Getting away from the city life and influences and being placed in the middle of nowhere might not have been on the list of your inner desires.

Golfers want to be in the middle of the green after a carefully placed hit. Moral of a golf story take time to examine each shot and share with those want who to learn the game. It's important to throw in some fun each time to gain the confidence necessary to overcome any obstacles.

Hopefully a golfer will continue to look back over the holes played from now and reminisce a little about the time they spent on the course. If you can look back and get a chuckle or two even better.

That's a grace of life saying yes to opportunities and seeing what happens. It was challenging watching other golfers and what happens naturally when they deprive themselves of strokes. **You all think of golfing as being "up there" but as someone said the distance from tee to green is not so much a matter of altitude as it is attitude.**

News this big is worth celebrating
Play the game as an Inspired Golfer

Remain **POSITIVE** on each course you play and a **RAINBOW** will surprise you.

AUTHOR BIO:

This author has many years of golf **experiences**. It is the brilliance that is brought forward in play. One never knows exactly where the golf ball will fly. That is what brings this story to life. My **concentration** throughout the game has educated my golfing techniques. The most exhilaration thing to remember is **relax** during a round of golf. My amateur status in this sport gives more stability to actual play. We all try to excel to the next level and actually this is accomplished as each person **remembers** the basics and those fun area's we passed thru during our learning years. Even the professional need a word of **encouragement** through these words. So, we must **do the best we can**. Our limits are what we impose upon ourselves.

The game of golf was drawing me to the fairway. Each time we attempted to follow the small ball it created words that produced a desire to explain this game to all who tried to conquer the "clang" at the bottom of a hole where a ball fell. The words will calm a golfer of all experience levels to the outdoor arena of this game.

This is the first published book from this author. Once the task is accomplished the shelves become full.

The desire to write words become overwhelming and the creation factor begins a new stream to follow.

Every slowdown in activity, the words flow.

Fred Grizzly
Author

Many words of encouragement for all types of golfers. There is room to grow one's experiences. Do not short change your golfing expertise.

~

The game of golf was drawing me to the fairway. Each time we attempted to follow the small ball it created words that produced a desire to explain this game to all who tried to conquer the "clang" at the bottom of a hole where a ball fell. The words used will give all types of golfers a picture of why so many people wanted to chase a little white object thru the fairways, woods, into the sand, and water, with the least amount of discomfort. Thus, empowering each golfer to swing with ease and watch the little object sail thru the air. All the rounds played over the years has brought to life the many challenges this game displays. There is always a happy ending to the game.